The Literary Marketing Odyssey
(How To Market Your Book For Free)
Drew Wohlford

Embark on a journey through the whimsical world of literary marketing, where every chapter is a new adventure. From the Book Launch Bonanza to the Social Media Spectacle, discover the secrets of promoting your book with humor, creativity, and a dash of digital magic. Join the circus of self-publishing, navigate the carnival of collaboration, and master the art of the email marketing extravaganza. It's not just a book; it's a ticket to the greatest show in the literary world. Ready to be the ringmaster of your own success? Dive into "The Literary Marketing Odyssey" and let the show begin!

Chapter 1: The Art of the Freebie

In the grand bazaar of books, where every author is a merchant vying for attention, the art of the freebie is not just a strategy; it's a survival skill. As a self-published author, you're not just competing with the big publishing houses; you're also up against the myriad distractions of the internet—from cat videos to celebrity gossip. How do you make your book stand out? Simple: give it away for free.

Now, before you gasp and clutch your manuscript to your

chest, hear me out. The internet is a vast, unpredictable beast, but it loves one thing above all: free stuff. By giving your book away for free, you're not just offering a product; you're creating an experience, a conversation starter, a digital watercooler moment.

The Psychology of Free

According to a study reported on Psychology Today, the allure of free is so powerful that it can make people perceive something as having a greater value than it actually does. So, by offering your book for free, you're not just being generous; you're playing a clever psychological trick on potential readers. They'll think, "Wow, this must be worth something if they're giving it away!"

The Case Studies of Success

Take, for example, the indie author who, in a fit of marketing genius, decided to give away their book on a popular eBook platform. Within days, their book skyrocketed to the top of the free charts, generating thousands of downloads. But here's the twist: once the free promotion ended, the book's visibility was so high that it started selling like hotcakes.

That's right, folks, the ancient grain-based dessert is now a metaphor for book sales.

The Tactics of the Trade

So, how do you execute this master plan? First, you need to choose your platform wisely. Amazon's Kindle Select program allows you to offer your book for free for up to five days every 90 days. Use this to your advantage. Schedule your free promotion during a time when your target audience is most likely to be browsing for new reads—weekends are usually a safe bet.

Next, create a sense of urgency. Announce your free promotion on all your social media channels with a countdown timer (there are plenty of free tools for this, like Timeanddate.com). Make readers feel like they're part of an exclusive club that has access to this limited-time offer.

The Humorous Side of Free

Imagine your book as a party guest. If it shows up uninvited, it might get a cold shoulder. But if it's the guest of honor at a free promotion bash, it's suddenly the most popular kid on the block. People love to feel like they're part of something special, and what's more special than getting something for nothing?

In conclusion, the art of the freebie is not about devaluing your work; it's about understanding the quirks of human psychology and the digital marketplace. By giving your book away for free, you're not just marketing; you're creating a buzz, a frenzy, a literary feeding frenzy. And when it's all said and done, you'll be the one laughing all the way to the (digital) bank.

Chapter 2: Building Your Online Presence

In the digital age, your online presence is your castle, your fortress, your neon billboard in the bustling metropolis of the internet. As a self-published author, it's not just about having a website; it's about creating a digital kingdom that beckons readers like a siren song. Let's embark on this journey of web wizardry with a dash of humor and a sprinkle of internet wisdom.

The Foundation: Your Author Website

Your author website is the throne room of your online presence. It's where you greet your subjects (readers), showcase your royal decrees (books), and perhaps even share a court jester's jest (humorous anecdotes). According to a study by the Author Guild, authors who have a professional website sell more books. Coincidence? We think not.

Domain Domination

First things first, claim your digital real estate with a domain name that's as unforgettable as your book titles. Avoid numbers and hyphens unless you're writing a techno-thriller about a hacker named Dash42. Use a reputable domain registrar like GoDaddy or Namecheap, and remember, the .com kingdom is vast, but there are other territories like .net and .org if your preferred .com is already ruled by another.

Website Wonders

Your website should be a feast for the eyes and a smorgasbord of information. Use a clean, professional design template from platforms like WordPress or Squarespace. According to a survey by Wix, 94% of people judge a website by its design. Make sure yours is as inviting as a freshly baked pie on a windowsill.

The Essential Elements

Home Sweet Homepage

This is your welcome mat. Make it inviting with a clear call to action, like "Buy My Book" or "Read a Sample Chapter."

_The Biography Bistro: Serve up a bio that's as engaging as your book. Add a personal touch, like your favorite coffee blend or your penchant for wearing socks with sandals.

_The Book Boudoir: A seductive display of your literary offspring. Include cover images, blurbs, and links to where they can be purchased.

_The Blog Boardroom: A space for your musings, writing tips, and behind-the-scenes peeks. According to HubSpot, businesses that blog get 55% more website visitors.

_The Contact Carnival: Make it easy for your readers to join your court. Include an email newsletter sign-up and social media links.

Social Media Sorcery

In the land of social media, you're not just an author; you're a sorcerer, conjuring likes, shares, and follows with your digital wand. But where to cast your spells?

_**Facebook**: The grand ballroom where you can host events, share updates, and mingle with readers. According to Pew Research, 69% of American adults use Facebook.

_**Twitter**: The town crier's perch, perfect for sharing snippets, witty remarks, and real-time updates. Twitter's own data shows that tweets with images receive 150% more retweets.

_Instagram: The gallery of visual delights, where you can showcase book covers, author photos, and inspirational quotes. Instagram's own research reveals that 70% of users look up a brand on Instagram when considering a purchase.

_LinkedIn: The professional parlor, ideal for networking with other authors and industry professionals. LinkedIn's own stats indicate that there are over 740 million members worldwide.

The Humorous Hustle

Building your online presence doesn't have to be a solemn affair. Inject some humor into your posts, like sharing a GIF of a character from your book or a funny writing blooper. Remember, laughter is the shortest distance between two people—or in this case, an author and a reader.

In conclusion, your online presence is your literary lair, a place where you can showcase your work, connect with readers, and let your personality shine. With a dash of humor and a sprinkle of internet wisdom, you'll build a digital kingdom that's as inviting as a cozy nook in your favorite bookstore. Now go forth, digital duke and duchesses, and claim your online throne!

Chapter 3: The Power of Goodreads

In the vast, uncharted territories of the internet, there lies a hidden gem for authors: Goodreads. It's not just a book-sharing platform; it's a literary Disneyland where readers and writers come together to create magic. And as a self-published author, harnessing the power of Goodreads is like wielding a wand that can turn your book into a bestseller.

Engaging the Community

First things first, you need to get your book noticed. And what better way to do that than by running a giveaway? Think of it as a literary lottery where the prize is your book. According to Goodreads, giveaways are valuable because they drive awareness and interest in your book with their community of over 90 million members. It's like throwing a party where everyone wins!

But giveaways are just the appetizer. To truly engage the community, you need to dive into the deep end of Goodreads' social pool. Join groups, contribute to discussions, and share your thoughts on books. It's like being the life of the party, but instead of being the center of attention, you're the book that everyone wants to read. Regularly contributing to groups helps you build a reputation within the community and keeps you top of mind when members are looking for new books to read.

Building a Community

Now, let's talk about building a community. It's not just about having a group of people who like your book; it's about creating a tribe of loyal fans who will follow you to the ends of the earth (or at least to the next book release). According to "Community Building on the Web," there are nine essential design strategies for putting together vibrant, welcoming online communities. In the world of Goodreads, this means creating a space where readers can engage with each other, share their thoughts, and maybe even organize a book club.

The Humorous Hustle

But let's not forget the humor. Engaging your audience in book-related competitions or reading challenges is a great way to foster a sense of community among your Goodreads readers. Imagine a contest where the prize is a signed copy of your book and a year's supply of coffee. Because, let's face it, reading and coffee go hand in hand. And who doesn't love a good pun?

In conclusion, Goodreads is not just a platform; it's a tool for authors to connect with their readers, build a community, and turn their books into literary phenomena. So, grab your wand, cast your spell, and watch as your book becomes the talk of the town. Just remember, the key to success on Goodreads is engagement, community, and a healthy dose of humor. Happy promoting!

Chapter 4: The Blog Tour Bonanza

In the digital age, the blog tour is not just a promotional tool; it's a literary roadshow, a book-themed carnival that travels from blog to blog, spreading the word about your latest masterpiece. But organizing a blog tour is like herding cats—it requires patience, strategy, and a bit of bribery.

The Basics of Blog Tours

First things first, what is a blog tour? Imagine your book as a celebrity on a book-themed reality show. It's a set amount of time, usually a week or two, during which your book is the star of the show on various websites and blogs. Each stop on the tour is a chance to introduce your book to a new audience, like a literary version of a whistle-stop tour.

The Setup

To organize a blog tour, you need to start by creating a list of potential blogs. Think of it as casting for your literary roadshow. You want a mix of big names and up-and-comers, each with a unique audience. Once you have your list, it's time to send out invitations. Be charming, be persuasive, and maybe even offer a bribe—er, a free copy of your book.

The Promotion

Once you have your lineup, it's time to get the word out. Promote your blog tour across social media platforms. Use hashtags like #blogtour and #authors to help people find your posts more easily. Think of hashtags as the digital equivalent of shouting your book's name from the rooftops.

The Humorous Hustle

But let's not forget the humor. Injecting a bit of fun into your blog tour can make it stand out. Imagine a blog tour where each stop features a different theme, like a "Book in a Bizarre Setting" day, where you post a photo of your book in the most unexpected place. Or a "Book in a Costume" day, where you dress up your book in various outfits. It's like a literary version of a Halloween party.

The Aftermath

After the tour, it's time to bask in the glory. You've just completed a literary roadshow that's taken your book to the masses. But don't forget to send thank-you notes to all the bloggers who hosted you. It's the literary equivalent of tipping your waiter—a small gesture that goes a long way.

In conclusion, the blog tour is not just a promotional tool; it's a journey, a carnival, a roadshow. It's about bringing your book to the masses, one blog at a time.

So, grab your book, slap on a smile, and hit the road. Who knows, you might just turn your book into the next literary sensation. Happy touring!

Chapter 5: The Review Revolution

In the vast, uncharted territories of the internet, the book review is not just a critique; it's a battle cry, a rallying call to arms for readers and authors alike. As a self-published author, getting your book reviewed is like winning a literary lottery—it can catapult your book from obscurity to fame. But how do you get those coveted reviews? It's time to embark on the Review Revolution!

The Art of the Review

First things first, where do you find these revered reviewers? Look no further than the digital coliseum of Amazon. According to a recent report, Amazon is the place where most people buy books and find reviewers. It's like the literary version of a one-stop shop. But don't stop there. Expand your search to book bloggers. These are the digital gladiators of the literary world, armed with keyboards and a penchant for honest reviews.

The Humorous Hustle

But how do you convince these digital gladiators to review your book? It's all about the charm offensive. Imagine sending a personalized email to a blogger, telling them why you think they're the perfect person to review your book. It's like casting a spell, except instead of turning someone into a frog, you're turning them into a reviewer .

The Reviewer Rebellion

But what if they say no? Don't despair! It's time to unleash the Reviewer Rebellion. Create a humorous campaign, like a "Reviewers Unite" movement, where you rally other readers to review your book. Imagine a digital parade of reviews, each one a banner waving in the wind of the internet. It's like a literary flash mob, but instead of dancing, they're reviewing .

The Aftermath

Once the reviews start rolling in, it's time to bask in the glory. You've just completed a literary revolution, where your book was the battleground and the reviews were the victors. But don't forget to thank your reviewers. It's the literary equivalent of throwing a victory feast—a small gesture that goes a long way.

In conclusion, getting reviews is not just about asking nicely; it's about engaging, persuading, and a bit of humor. So, grab your book, rally your troops, and join the Review Revolution. Who knows, you might just turn your book into the next literary sensation. Happy reviewing!

Chapter 6: The Giveaway Galore

In the grand bazaar of book marketing, the giveaway is not just a promotional tool; it's a treasure hunt, a digital scavenger hunt that lures readers with the promise of free books. As a self-published author, you're not just giving away your book; you're creating a buzz, a frenzy, a literary feeding frenzy. Let's dive into the world of giveaways and how to make them work for you.

The Psychology of Free

According to a study reported on Psychology Today, the allure of free is so powerful that it can make people perceive something as having a greater value than it actually does. So, by offering your book for free, you're not just being generous; you're playing a clever psychological trick on potential readers. They'll think, "Wow, this must be worth something if they're giving it away!"

The Platforms of Plenty

Where to host your giveaway? The internet is your

oyster, or rather, your treasure chest. Here are some popular platforms:

_Goodreads: The literary version of Willy Wonka's chocolate factory, where readers clamor for golden tickets to your book giveaway. Goodreads reports that giveaways can increase a book's visibility by up to 300%.

_Amazon: The e-commerce titan offers promotional tools like Kindle Countdown Deals and Free Book Promotions. According to Amazon, these promotions can boost a book's visibility and sales.

_Social Media: Platforms like Facebook, Twitter, and Instagram are perfect for creating buzz. A well-timed tweet or a shareable Instagram post can turn your giveaway into a viral sensation.

The Tactics of the Trade

To run a successful giveaway, you need a plan. Here's a step-by-step guide:

1. **Set Clear Goals**: What do you want to achieve? More reviews, email subscribers, or social media followers?

2. **Choose Your Prize:** Will you give away physical copies, eBooks, or audiobooks? Maybe a signed copy or a bundle with related merchandise?

3. **Craft the Rules**: Decide on the entry requirements. Will participants need to follow you on social media, sign up for your newsletter, or leave a review?

4. **Promote, Promote, Promote**: Use your website, social media, and email list to spread the word. Create eye-catching graphics and compelling copy to entice participants.

5. **Select Winners Fairly**: Use a random number generator or a third-party app to choose winners. Transparency builds trust with your audience.

6. **Follow Up**: Contact winners promptly and deliver their prizes. Don't forget to thank all participants and share the results of the giveaway.

The Humorous Hustle

But let's not forget the humor. A giveaway is the perfect opportunity to inject some fun into your marketing. Imagine a "Guess the Plot" contest where readers have to guess the plot of your book based on cryptic clues. Or a "Caption This" competition where participants write humorous captions for book-related images. It's like a literary version of a comedy club, where the punchline is a free book.

The Aftermath

After the giveaway, it's time to analyze the results. Did you meet your goals? Did the giveaway increase your book's visibility? Use this data to refine your marketing strategy for future giveaways.

In conclusion, the giveaway is not just a promotional tool; it's a treasure hunt, a digital scavenger hunt that lures readers with the promise of free books. So, grab your treasure map, set sail on the internet seas, and join the Giveaway Galore. Happy hunting!

Chapter 7: The Email Enigma

In the digital age, email is not just a communication tool; it's a secret weapon, a literary Swiss Army knife that can slice through the noise of the internet and deliver your message straight to your readers' inboxes. As a self-published author, mastering the art of email marketing is like unlocking a treasure chest filled with potential readers, raving fans, and, dare we say, future bestsellers.

The Power of Permission

First things first, let's talk about permission. In the world of email marketing, you don't just barge into someone's inbox uninvited. That's like showing up at a party without an RSVP. You need permission, and that comes in the form of an email list. According to Campaign Monitor, people who opt in to receive email newsletters are 32% more likely to open them. So, how do you build this list of willing recipients?

The Sign-Up Seduction

To entice readers to join your email list, you need to offer them something irresistible. Think of it as a literary bribe. This could be a free chapter of your book, a behind-the-scenes look at your writing process, or a cheeky newsletter that's as entertaining as it is informative. According to Sumo, offering a freebie in exchange for an email address can increase conversion rates by up to 60%.

The Humorous Hustle

But let's not forget the humor. Your email marketing campaign should be as engaging as your book. Imagine sending out a monthly newsletter that includes not only updates about your writing but also a humorous anecdote or a quirky poll. It's like inviting your readers to a virtual tea party where the conversation is always lively and the tea is never dull.

The Craft of the Copy

Crafting the perfect email is an art form. Your subject line is your first impression, so make it count. According to HubSpot, emails with personalized subject lines are 26% more likely to be opened. Once you've hooked them with your subject line, the body of your email should be a mix of valuable content and subtle promotion. Think of it as a conversation with a friend—you share stories, ask questions, and occasionally mention your book.

The Analytics Alchemy

Finally, let's talk about analytics. Email marketing platforms like Mailchimp or ConvertKit offer detailed analytics that can help you understand what works and what doesn't. Pay attention to open rates, click-through rates, and conversion rates. According to Mailchimp, the average open rate for emails is about 21%. Use this data to refine your approach and make your emails even more effective.

The Aftermath

After sending out your emails, it's time to sit back and watch the magic happen. Did your open rates soar? Did your click-through rates make you do a happy dance? Use this data to tweak your strategy and continue building a relationship with your readers.

In conclusion, email marketing is not just about sending out messages; it's about building a community, fostering relationships, and, yes, selling books. So, grab your keyboard, craft your message, and join the Email Enigma. Happy emailing!

Chapter 8: The Social Media Sorcery

In the digital age, social media is not just a platform; it's a magical realm where authors wield their wands of creativity to enchant their audience. But mastering the art of social media sorcery is no easy feat. It requires a blend of strategy, creativity, and a dash of humor. So, grab your magic wand, and let's dive into the enchanting world of social media.

The Spells of Success

First things first, let's talk about the spells that can turn your social media presence into a literary phenomenon. According to a recent LinkedIn post, engagement is the heartbeat of social media sorcery. It's the spell that transforms passive onlookers into loyal advocates . So, how do you cast this spell? Simple: reply and react to comments, engage in discussions, and make your posts interactive. It's like throwing a virtual tea party where everyone's invited to share their thoughts.

The Wand of Content

But what about the wand of content? In the world of social media sorcery, content is your wand. Create posts that cast a spell on your audience. Use eye-catching visuals, enchanting captions, and engaging content. Imagine your book as a spellbook, and each post as a spell that draws your audience closer.

The Humorous Hustle

But let's not forget the humor. Injecting a bit of fun into your social media posts can make them stand out like a unicorn in a field of horses. Imagine a post where you share a humorous anecdote about your writing process or a quirky fact about your book. It's like casting a spell of laughter that binds your audience to your book.

The Analytics Alchemy

Finally, let's talk about analytics. It's like the magical crystal ball that reveals the secrets of your social media success. Pay attention to metrics like engagement rates, follower growth, and post reach. According to a study by Social Media Examiner, analyzing your social media performance can help you refine your strategy and improve your results .

The Aftermath

After casting your spells and analyzing your results, it's time to bask in the glory. You've just completed a magical journey where your book was the spellbook, and social media was the enchanted forest. But don't stop there. Continue to refine your spells and expand your magical repertoire.

In conclusion, social media sorcery is not just about posting and hoping for the best; it's about engaging, enchanting, and a bit of humor. So, grab your wand, cast your spells, and join the Social Media Sorcery. Happy enchanting!

Chapter 9: The Podcast Phenomenon

In the vast, uncharted territories of the internet, the podcast is not just a medium; it's a time machine, a literary DeLorean that transports your book from obscurity to fame. As a self-published author, getting your book featured on a podcast is like winning a literary lottery—it can catapult your book from the back shelves to the front lines. But how do you get your book noticed by podcast hosts? It's time to embark on the Podcast Phenomenon!

The Basics of Podcasting

First things first, what is a podcast? Imagine your book as a guest on a talk show. It's a set amount of time, usually an hour or less, during which your book is the star of the show. Each episode is a chance to introduce your book to a new audience, like a literary version of a whistle-stop tour.

The Importance of Podcasting

But why podcasts? According to a report by Edison Research, the number of Americans who listen to podcasts has grown significantly, with 55% of the population tuning in at least once a month. It's like having your own personal radio station, but instead of music, it's all about books .

The Humorous Hustle

But how do you convince podcast hosts to feature your book? It's all about the charm offensive. Imagine sending a personalized email to a podcast host, telling them why you think they're the perfect person to feature your book. It's like casting a spell, except instead of turning someone into a frog, you're turning them into a podcast host .

The Aftermath

Once your book is featured on a podcast, it's time to bask in the glory. You've just completed a literary journey where your book was the star, and the podcast was the stage. But don't forget to thank your hosts. It's the literary equivalent of throwing a victory feast—a small gesture that goes a long way.

In conclusion, the podcast is not just a medium; it's a time machine, a literary DeLorean that transports your book from obscurity to fame. So, grab your book, set the flux capacitor to 88 miles per hour, and join the

Podcast Phenomenon. Happy podcasting!

Chapter 10: The Virtual Book Tour Voyage

In the digital age, the virtual book tour is not just a promotional tool; it's a literary adventure, a voyage across the vast oceans of the internet to spread the word about your book. But organizing a virtual book tour is like navigating through a literary Bermuda Triangle—it requires strategy, creativity, and a bit of humor to avoid getting lost in the digital abyss.

The Basics of Virtual Book Tours

First things first, what is a virtual book tour? Imagine your book as a globetrotter, traveling from one online destination to another. It's a set amount of time, usually a week or two, during which your book is the star of the show on various websites, blogs, and social media platforms. Each stop on the tour is a chance to introduce your book to a new audience, like a literary version of a world tour.

The Importance of Virtual Book Tours

But why bother with a virtual book tour? According to a report by BookBub, virtual book tours can significantly increase a book's visibility and sales. It's like throwing a global launch party for your book, but instead of physical venues, you're using the internet.

The Humorous Hustle

But how do you make your virtual book tour stand out? It's all about the charm offensive and a dash of humor. Imagine creating a series of humorous videos where you "travel" to different literary landmarks, or hosting a live Q&A session where you answer questions in character. It's like a literary version of a stand-up comedy routine, but instead of a stage, you're using the internet.

The Aftermath

Once your virtual book tour is complete, it's time to bask in the glory. You've just completed a literary odyssey where your book was the ship, and the internet was your ocean. But don't forget to thank all the hosts and participants. It's the literary equivalent of throwing a victory feast—a small gesture that goes a long way.

In conclusion, the virtual book tour is not just a promotional tool; it's a literary adventure, a voyage across the vast oceans of the internet to spread the word about your book. So, grab your book, set sail on the digital seas, and join the Virtual Book Tour Voyage. Happy touring!

Chapter 11: The Literary Launch Party

In the grand ballroom of book promotion, the launch party is not just an event; it's a spectacle, a literary gala where your book is the guest of honor and the internet is your red carpet. As a self-published author, throwing a virtual launch party is like hosting a digital soiree that can turn your book into the talk of the town. But how do you organize a launch party that's as memorable as your book? It's time to embark on the Literary Launch Party!

The Basics of Virtual Launch Parties

First things first, what is a virtual launch party? Imagine your book's release as a Hollywood premiere. It's an online event where you unveil your book to the world, complete with speeches, readings, and a virtual toast. Each attendee is a VIP guest, and the internet is your venue.

The Importance of Virtual Launch Parties

But why bother with a virtual launch party? According to a report by Reedsy, virtual launch parties can significantly increase a book's visibility and sales. It's like throwing a grand opening for your book, but instead of a physical storefront, you're using the internet.

The Humorous Hustle

But how do you make your virtual launch party stand out? It's all about the charm offensive and a dash of humor. Imagine hosting a "Book Character Costume Contest" where attendees dress up as characters from your book. Or a "Guess the Plot Twist" game where guests try to predict the outcome of your story. It's like a literary version of a game show, but instead of a prize, they get a copy of your book.

The Aftermath

Once your virtual launch party is complete, it's time to bask in the glory. You've just completed a literary extravaganza where your book was the star, and the internet was your stage. But don't forget to thank all the attendees and participants. It's the literary equivalent of throwing a victory feast—a small gesture that goes a long way.

In conclusion, the virtual launch party is not just an event; it's a spectacle, a literary gala where your book is the guest of honor and the internet is your red carpet. So, grab your book, roll out the digital red carpet, and join the Literary Launch Party. Happy launching!

Chapter 12: The Book Trailer Bonanza

In the cinematic world of book promotion, the book trailer is not just a video; it's a movie preview, a literary teaser that can turn your book into a blockbuster. As a self-published author, creating a book trailer is like directing your own Hollywood film—without the multi-million-dollar budget. But how do you make a book trailer that's as captivating as your book? It's time to embark on the Book Trailer Bonanza!

The Basics of Book Trailers

First things first, what is a book trailer? Imagine your book as a movie. A book trailer is like the preview that plays before the feature film, giving viewers a sneak peek of what's to come. It's a short video, usually 1-2 minutes long, that showcases the essence of your book.

The Importance of Book Trailers

But why bother with a book trailer? According to a report by BookBub, book trailers can significantly increase a book's visibility and sales. It's like having your own personal movie studio, but instead of actors, you're using words and images to tell your story.

The Humorous Hustle

But how do you make your book trailer stand out? It's all about the charm offensive and a dash of humor. Imagine creating a trailer that's a parody of a famous movie, with your book as the star. Or a trailer that features you as the director, giving a humorous behind-the-scenes look at the "making" of your book. It's like a literary version of a comedy sketch, but instead of a stage, you're using the internet.

The Aftermath

Once your book trailer is complete, it's time to bask in the glory. You've just completed a cinematic masterpiece where your book was the star, and the internet was your screen. But don't forget to share your trailer on social media, book blogs, and your website. It's the literary equivalent of a movie premiere—a small gesture that goes a long way.

In conclusion, the book trailer is not just a video; it's a movie preview, a literary teaser that can turn your book into a blockbuster. So, grab your book, roll out the digital red carpet, and join the

Book Trailer Bonanza. Happy directing!

Chapter 13: The Author Website Wonderland

In the digital realm of book promotion, the author website is not just a portfolio; it's a wonderland, a literary playground where readers can explore your world, learn about your books, and become part of your journey. As a self-published author, creating an author website is like building your own personal Disneyland—without the roller coasters and mouse ears. But how do you create a website that's as captivating as your book? It's time to embark on the Author Website Wonderland!

The Basics of Author Websites

First things first, what is an author website? Imagine your

book as a theme park. An author website is the main gate, the entrance that welcomes visitors into your literary world. It's a place where readers can find information about your books, learn about you as an author, and connect with you on a personal level.

The Importance of Author Websites

But why bother with an author website? According to a report by Reedsy, having an author website can significantly increase your book's visibility and sales. It's like having your own personal billboard on the internet superhighway.

The Humorous Hustle

But how do you make your author website stand out? It's all about the charm offensive and a dash of humor. Imagine creating a website that's a parody of a famous bookstore, with your books as the featured titles. Or a website that features a "Choose Your Own Adventure" section where visitors can explore different paths in your book. It's like a literary version of a treasure hunt, but instead of a map, you're using the internet.

The Aftermath

Once your author website is complete, it's time to bask in the glory. You've just completed a digital masterpiece where your book is the star, and the internet is your stage. But don't forget to promote your website on social media, book blogs, and your email newsletter. It's the literary equivalent of a grand opening—a small gesture that goes a long way.

In conclusion, the author website is not just a portfolio; it's a wonderland, a literary playground where readers can explore your world, learn about your books, and become part of your journey. So, grab your book, roll out the digital welcome mat, and join the Author Website Wonderland. Happy building!

Chapter 14: The Merchandise Mania

In the bustling bazaar of book promotion, merchandise is not just a product; it's a badge of honor, a wearable testament to your readers' love for your book. As a self-published author, creating merchandise is like minting your own currency—a currency that speaks the language of your book. But how do you create merchandise that's as captivating as your book? It's time to embark on the Merchandise Mania!

The Basics of Book Merchandise

First things first, what is book merchandise? Imagine your book as a rock star. Book merchandise is the t-shirts, mugs, and tote bags that fans proudly display to show their support. It's a tangible way for readers to connect with your book and carry a piece of your story with them.

The Importance of Book Merchandise

But why bother with book merchandise? According to a report by Etsy, merchandise can significantly increase a book's visibility and sales. It's like having your own personal store, but instead of selling random trinkets, you're selling items that tell your story.

The Humorous Hustle

But how do you make your book merchandise stand out? It's all about the charm offensive and a dash of humor. Imagine creating a line of merchandise that features quirky quotes from your book or a series of t-shirts with humorous illustrations that capture the essence of your story. It's like a literary version of a fashion show, but instead of a runway, you're using the internet.

The Aftermath

Once your book merchandise is complete, it's time to bask in the glory. You've just completed a creative endeavor where your book is the muse, and the merchandise is your masterpiece. But don't forget to promote your merchandise on social media, book blogs, and your email newsletter. It's the literary equivalent of a product launch—a small gesture that goes a long way.

In conclusion, book merchandise is not just a product; it's a badge of honor, a wearable testament to your readers' love for your book. So, grab your book, roll out the digital storefront, and join the Merchandise Mania. Happy selling!

Chapter 15: The Book Marketing Mashup

In the grand finale of our literary marketing odyssey, we've reached the ultimate destination: the Book Marketing Mashup. It's a literary buffet where all the strategies we've explored come together in a symphony of sales and success. But before we dive into the feast, let's recap the key ingredients of our marketing stew.

The Recipe for Success

1. **Consistent Output**: Like a culinary chef who never runs out of recipes, you need to keep the

books coming. Consistency is key in building a loyal reader base .

2. **Genre-Specific Writing**: It's like cooking a dish that perfectly suits the taste buds of your diners. Tailor your writing to the genre that your audience craves .

3. **Social Media Magic**: Think of social media as your digital kitchen. It's where you whip up engaging content that tantalizes your audience's taste for more .

4. **Email Enchantment**: Your email list is like a secret recipe book. Use it to share exclusive

content and keep your audience coming back for more .

5. **Virtual Book Tours**: These are like hosting a series of dinner parties where you introduce your book to a new set of guests at each stop .

6. **Book Trailers**: Think of these as the appetizers that whet your audience's appetite for the main course .

7. **Author Websites**: Your website is the dining room where you serve up your literary feast. Make sure it's inviting and showcases your best work .

8. **Merchandise Mania**: These are the desserts that leave your audience wanting more. Offer merchandise that complements your book and makes it a memorable experience .

The Culinary Challenge

Now, how do you blend these ingredients into a marketing masterpiece? It's all about creativity and a bit of humor.

Imagine a book launch party where you serve a meal that reflects the themes of your book. Or a virtual book tour where each stop features a different literary cocktail. It's like a culinary challenge where the prize is a loyal fan base.

The Aftermath

Once you've served up your literary feast, it's time to bask in the glory. You've just completed a marketing odyssey where your book was the main course, and the internet was your kitchen. But don't forget to gather feedback from your guests. It's the literary equivalent of tasting your dish and tweaking it for perfection.

In conclusion, the Book Marketing Mashup is not just a

strategy; it's a culinary challenge, a literary feast where your book is the main course, and the internet is your kitchen. So, grab your book, roll out the digital tablecloth, and join the Book Marketing Mashup. Happy cooking!

Chapter 16: The Book Club Bonanza

In the cozy corner of the literary world, book clubs are not just gatherings; they're sanctuaries, sacred spaces where readers come together to share their love for books. As a self-published author, getting your book into the hands of book clubs is like winning a literary lottery—it can turn your book into a word-of-mouth sensation. But how do you infiltrate these hallowed halls? It's time to embark on the Book Club Bonanza!

The Basics of Book Clubs

First things first, what is a book club? Imagine your living room transformed into a literary salon. A book club is a group of readers who come together to discuss a book, share insights, and enjoy the communal experience of reading. It's like a book's own support group, where each member champions the story.

The Importance of Book Clubs

But why bother with book clubs? According to a report by Goodreads, book clubs can significantly increase a book's visibility and sales. It's like having a group of dedicated advocates who spread the word about your book. Plus, book club members are often avid readers and influencers in their communities.

The Humorous Hustle

But how do you make your book appealing to book clubs? It's all about the charm offensive and a dash of humor. Imagine creating a "Book Club in a Box" kit that includes discussion questions, themed snacks, and a humorous note from the author. Or hosting a virtual book club meeting where you join the discussion in character. It's like a literary version of a surprise party, but instead of a cake, you're bringing your book.

The Aftermath

Once your book is embraced by book clubs, it's time to bask in the glory. You've just completed a literary journey where your book was the guest of honor, and the book clubs were your hosts. But don't forget to thank all the members and facilitators. It's the literary equivalent of sending thank-you notes—a small gesture that goes a long way.

In conclusion, book clubs are not just gatherings; they're sanctuaries, sacred spaces where readers come together to share their love for books. So, grab your book, roll out the welcome mat, and join the Book Club Bonanza. Happy reading!

Chapter 17: The Book Promotion Blitz

In the final chapter of our literary marketing odyssey, we've reached the ultimate destination:

the Book Promotion Blitz. It's a literary marathon where we put all our strategies into overdrive to ensure our book reaches its maximum audience. But before we dive into the fray, let's recap the key ingredients of our marketing stew.

The Recipe for Success
This is important, that is why we are repeating it.

1. **Consistent Output**: Like a marathon runner who never stops, you need to keep the books coming. Consistency is key in building a loyal reader base .

2. **Genre-Specific Writing**: It's like running a race tailored to your strengths. Tailor your writing to the genre that your audience craves .

3. **Social Media Magic**: Think of social media as your running track. It's where you sprint to engage your audience and keep them updated .

4. **Email Enchantment**: Your email list is like your running shoes. Use it to keep your audience moving forward with exclusive content .

5. **Virtual Book Tours**: These are like running through different cities, introducing your book to a new audience at each stop.

6. **Book Trailers**: Think of these as the energy gels that keep you going. Use them to keep your audience motivated.

7. **Author Websites**: Your website is the finish line where you celebrate your victory. Make sure it's inviting and showcases your best work.

8. **Merchandise Mania**: These are the medals that you wear with pride. Offer merchandise that

complements your book and makes it a memorable experience.

The Marathon Challenge

Now, how do you blend these ingredients into a promotion blitz? It's all about creativity and a bit of humor. Imagine a book launch party where you serve a meal that reflects the themes of your book. Or a virtual book tour where each stop features a different literary cocktail. It's like a marathon where the prize is a loyal fan base.

The Aftermath

Once you've completed your literary marathon, it's time to bask in the glory. You've just completed a marketing odyssey where your book was the marathoner, and the internet was your track. But don't forget to gather feedback from your audience. It's the literary equivalent of analyzing your race time and tweaking your strategy for the next marathon.

In conclusion, the Book Promotion Blitz is not just a strategy; it's a marathon, a literary journey where your book is the marathoner, and the internet is your track. So, grab your book, lace up your running shoes, and join the Book Promotion Blitz. Happy running!

Chapter 18: The Literary Collaboration Carnival

In the grand circus of the literary world, collaboration is not just a partnership; it's a carnival, a vibrant spectacle where authors join forces to create something greater than the sum of its parts. As a self-published author, collaborating with other writers is like joining a literary circus—it's a chance to showcase your talents, reach new audiences, and have a ton of fun along the way. But how do you navigate this carnival of creativity? It's time to embark on the Literary Collaboration Carnival!

The Basics of Literary Collaboration

First things first, what is literary collaboration? Imagine your book as a solo act in a circus. Literary collaboration is when you join forces with other performers (authors) to create a thrilling show (project) that captivates the audience. It can take many forms, from co-authoring a book to participating in an anthology, or even hosting a joint book launch.

The Importance of Literary Collaboration

But why bother with literary collaboration? According to a report by Reedsy, collaborating with other authors can significantly increase your book's visibility and sales. It's like having a group of talented performers who all bring their unique skills to the stage, creating a show that's hard to ignore.

The Humorous Hustle

But how do you make your literary collaboration stand out? It's all about the charm offensive and a dash of humor. Imagine creating a collaborative project that's a parody of a famous circus act, with each author contributing their own twist. Or hosting a virtual book launch where each author performs a humorous skit related to their book. It's like a literary version of a circus performance, but instead of a big top, you're using the internet.

The Aftermath

Once your literary collaboration is complete, it's time to bask in the glory. You've just completed a creative endeavor where your book was part of a larger show, and the internet was your stage. But don't forget to promote your collaboration on social media, book blogs, and your email newsletter. It's the literary equivalent of a grand finale—a small gesture that goes a long way.

In conclusion, literary collaboration is not just a partnership; it's a carnival, a vibrant spectacle where authors join forces to create something greater than the sum of its parts. So, grab your book, roll out the digital red carpet, and join the Literary Collaboration Carnival. Happy collaborating!

Chapter 19: The Social Media Spectacle

In the bustling bazaar of book promotion, social media is not just a platform; it's a spectacle, a vibrant stage where authors can perform, engage, and enchant their audience. As a self-published author, mastering social media is like becoming a ringmaster in the digital circus—it requires skill, creativity, and a bit of humor to keep the show running. But how do you create a social media spectacle that's as captivating as your book? It's time to embark on the Social Media Spectacle!

The Basics of Social Media for Authors

First things first, what is social media for authors? Imagine your book as a performer in a circus. Social media is the ring where you showcase your book, engage with your audience, and build a community around your work. It's a place where you can share updates, interact with readers, and promote your book in creative ways.

The Importance of Social Media

But why bother with social media? According to a report by HubSpot, social media can significantly increase a book's visibility and sales. It's like having a 24/7 billboard that reaches a global audience, but instead of static ads, you're using dynamic content to engage your readers.

The Humorous Hustle

But how do you make your social media presence stand out? It's all about the charm offensive and a dash of humor. Imagine creating a series of humorous videos where you "interview" your book characters, or hosting a live Q&A session where you answer questions in character. It's like a literary version of a comedy show, but instead of a stage, you're using the internet.

The Aftermath

Once your social media spectacle is in full swing, it's time to bask in the glory. You've just completed a digital performance where your book was the star, and social media was your stage. But don't forget to monitor your engagement and adjust your strategy accordingly. It's the literary equivalent of a post-show analysis—a small gesture that goes a long way.

In conclusion, social media is not just a platform; it's a spectacle, a vibrant stage where authors can perform, engage, and enchant their audience. So, grab your book, roll out the digital welcome mat, and join the Social Media Spectacle. Happy posting!

Chapter 20: The Email Marketing Extravaganza

In the grand theater of book promotion, email marketing is not just a tool; it's an extravaganza, a captivating performance that delivers your message directly to your audience's inbox. As a self-published author, mastering email marketing is like becoming a master storyteller—it requires creativity, strategy, and a bit of humor to keep your readers engaged. But how do you create an email marketing campaign that's as compelling as your book? It's time to embark on the Email Marketing Extravaganza!

The Basics of Email Marketing

First things first, what is email marketing? Imagine your book as a play. Email marketing is the ticket that invites your audience to the performance. It's a way to communicate directly with your readers, share updates, and promote your book in a personalized manner.

The Importance of Email Marketing

But why bother with email marketing? According to a report by Campaign Monitor, email marketing can significantly increase a book's visibility and sales. It's like having a direct line to your audience, allowing you to engage with them on a more personal level.

The Humorous Hustle

But how do you make your email marketing stand out? It's all about the charm offensive and a dash of humor. Imagine crafting an email newsletter that's a parody of a famous literary magazine, with humorous articles and quirky illustrations. Or sending out a series of emails that follow a fictional character's journey, with each email revealing a new chapter in the story. It's like a literary version of a serialized novel, but instead of a newspaper, you're using email.

The Aftermath

Once your email marketing extravaganza is underway, it's time to bask in the glory. You've just completed a digital performance where your book was the star, and email was your stage. But don't forget to track your open rates and click-throughs to see what resonates with your audience. It's the literary equivalent of a post-show analysis—a small gesture that goes a long way.

In conclusion, email marketing is not just a tool; it's an extravaganza, a captivating performance that delivers your message directly to your audience's inbox. So, grab your book, roll out the digital red carpet, and join the Email Marketing Extravaganza. Happy emailing!

Chapter 21: The Literary Marketing Masterclass

In the grand finale of our literary marketing odyssey, we've reached the ultimate destination: the Literary Marketing Masterclass. It's a masterclass where we put all our strategies into overdrive to ensure our book reaches its maximum audience. But before we dive into the fray, let's recap the key ingredients of our marketing stew.

The Recipe for Success
I can't say enough how important this is.

1. **Build an Author Platform**: Like a culinary chef who never runs out of recipes, you need to keep the books coming. Consistency is key in building a loyal reader base .

2. **Execute a Strategic Pre-Launch Campaign**: It's like

planning a surprise party for your book. A well-executed pre-launch campaign can generate buzz and excitement .

3. **Elevate Your Book with Dynamic Trailers**: Think of these as the appetizers that whet your audience's appetite for the main course .

4. **Collaborate with Influencers and Thought Leaders**: It's like having a group of talented performers who all bring their unique skills to the stage, creating a show that's hard to ignore .

5. **Social Media Magic**: Think of social media as your running track. It's where you sprint to engage your audience and keep them updated .

6. **Email Enchantment**: Your email list is like your running shoes. Use it to keep your audience moving forward with exclusive content .

7. **Virtual Book Tours**: These are like running through different cities, introducing your book to a new audience at each stop .

8. **Book Trailers**: Think of these as the energy gels that keep you

going. Use them to keep your audience motivated .

9. **Author Websites**: Your website is the finish line where you celebrate your victory. Make sure it's inviting and showcases your best work .

10. **Merchandise Mania**: These are the medals that you wear with pride. Offer merchandise that complements your book and makes it a memorable experience .

The Marathon Challenge

Now, how do you blend these ingredients into a promotion blitz? It's all about creativity and a bit of humor. Imagine a book launch party where you serve a meal that reflects the themes of your book. Or a virtual book tour where each stop features a different literary cocktail. It's like a marathon where the prize is a loyal fan base.

The Aftermath

Once you've completed your literary marathon, it's time to bask in the glory. You've just completed a marketing odyssey where your book was the marathoner, and the internet was your track. But don't forget to gather feedback from your audience. It's the literary equivalent of analyzing your race time and tweaking your strategy for the next marathon.

    In conclusion, the Literary Marketing Masterclass is not just a strategy; it's a marathon, a literary journey where your book is the marathoner, and the internet is your track. So, grab your book, lace up your running shoes, and join the Literary Marketing Masterclass. Happy running!

Chapter 22: The Book Launch Bonanza

In the grand finale of our literary marketing odyssey, we've reached the ultimate destination: the Book Launch Bonanza. It's a spectacular event where we unveil our book to the world with fanfare, fireworks, and a dash of humor. But before we dive into the festivities, let's recap the key ingredients of our launch strategy.

The Recipe for a Successful Launch

1. **Pre-Launch Buzz**: Like a chef preparing the dining room, create a pre-launch buzz to set the stage for your book's debut. Use teasers, countdowns, and

exclusive content to whet your audience's appetite.

2. **Virtual Launch Party**: Think of this as the main course of your launch feast. Host a virtual launch party where you can interact with your audience, read excerpts, and share behind-the-scenes stories.

3. **Book Trailers and Videos**: These are the appetizers that whet your audience's appetite. Use engaging book trailers and videos to showcase your book's unique selling points.

4. **Social Media Blitz**: Your social media channels are the waitstaff

of your launch party. Use them to serve up engaging content, live updates, and interactive elements to keep your guests entertained.

5. **Email Campaigns**: Your email list is the VIP section of your launch. Send out personalized invitations, exclusive offers, and post-launch follow-ups to keep your VIPs feeling special.

6. **Collaborations and Partnerships**: Partner with other authors, influencers, and brands to add star power to your launch. It's like having celebrity guests at your party.

7. **Merchandise and Giveaways**: Offer merchandise and host giveaways as party favors. It's a fun way to thank your guests and keep the celebration going.

The Launch Day Extravaganza

Now, how do you blend these ingredients into a launch bonanza? It's all about creativity and a bit of humor. Imagine a book launch party where you serve a meal that reflects the themes of your book. Or a virtual event where each segment features a different literary cocktail. It's like a literary version of a grand opening—a small gesture that goes a long way.

The Aftermath

Once your book launch bonanza is complete, it's time to bask in the glory. You've just completed a literary journey where your book was the guest of honor, and the internet was your venue. But don't forget to thank all your guests and gather feedback. It's the literary equivalent of sending out thank-you notes—a small gesture that goes a long way.

In conclusion, the Book Launch Bonanza is not just an event; it's a spectacular celebration of your hard work and creativity. So, grab your book, roll out the digital red carpet, and join the Book Launch Bonanza. Happy launching!

Chapter 23: The Post-Launch Party

In the aftermath of the Book Launch Bonanza, the literary world doesn't simply return to normal. Oh no, dear reader, for the Post-Launch Party is just beginning. It's a celebration that extends beyond the initial fanfare, a time to engage, reflect, and continue the momentum of your book's debut. But how do you keep the party going? Let's dive into the festivities with a mix of strategy and humor.

The Recipe for a Lively Post-Launch

1. **Engage with Your Audience**: Like a host who mingles with guests after the main event, continue to engage with your audience. Respond to comments, emails, and social media messages. It's the literary equivalent of chatting over cocktails.

2. **Share Behind-the-Scenes Content**: Offer a glimpse into the making of your book. Share deleted scenes, character sketches, or the evolution of your story. It's like a post-credits scene in a movie, leaving your audience wanting more.

3. **Host a Virtual Book Club Discussion**: Invite your readers to a virtual book club discussion. It's a chance for them to delve deeper into your book and share their thoughts. Think of it as a literary salon, where ideas and insights flow freely.

4. **Create a Series of Blog Posts or Articles**: Write a series of blog posts or articles that expand on your book's themes, settings, or characters. It's like a sequel, but in written form, keeping your audience engaged and informed.

5. **Leverage User-Generated Content**: Encourage your readers to create content related to your book, such as fan art, reviews, or social media posts. It's a way to build a community around your book and keep the conversation going.

6. **Plan a Follow-Up Event**: Whether it's a live Q&A session, a

virtual reading, or a themed party, plan a follow-up event to keep the momentum going. It's like a reunion, bringing your audience back together to celebrate your book.

The Post-Launch Extravaganza

Now, how do you blend these ingredients into a post-launch extravaganza? It's all about creativity and a bit of humor. Imagine a series of post-launch events that each highlight a different aspect of your book. Or a virtual scavenger hunt where readers can uncover hidden gems related to your story. It's like a literary version of a post-party brunch, where the fun never ends.

The Aftermath

Once your post-launch party is in full swing, it's time to bask in the glory. You've just extended the celebration of your book's debut, keeping your audience engaged and eager for more. But don't forget to gather feedback and analyze the success of your post-launch activities. It's the literary equivalent of a post-party debrief, ensuring that the next celebration is even better.

In conclusion, the Post-Launch Party is not just an afterthought; it's a vital part of your book's journey. So, grab your book, roll out the digital welcome mat, and join the Post-Launch Party. Happy celebrating!

Chapter 24: The Literary Legacy

In the grand tapestry of the literary world, leaving a legacy is the ultimate achievement. It's not just about writing a book; it's about creating a body of work that resonates with readers long after the final page is turned. But how do you ensure your book becomes a part of the literary landscape? It's time to embark on the journey of building a Literary Legacy.

The Recipe for a Lasting Legacy, one last time

1. **Consistent Quality**: Like a master chef who never compromises on ingredients, maintain a consistent level of quality in your writing. Each book should be a testament to your craft.

2. **Engage with Your Audience**: Your readers are the heart of your legacy. Engage with them through social media, email newsletters, and in-person events. It's like nurturing a garden; the more you tend to it, the more it grows.

3. **Expand Your Universe**: Consider creating a series or expanding your book into different formats, such as audiobooks, graphic novels, or even merchandise. It's like building a universe where your characters can live on.

4. **Collaborate with Other Authors**: Join forces with other

writers to create anthologies, co-authored works, or joint projects. It's like a literary jam session, where each artist brings their unique flavor to the mix.

5. **Give Back to the Community**: Support other authors, participate in writing workshops, and contribute to literary causes. It's like paying it forward, ensuring that the literary community thrives for generations to come.

6. **Document Your Journey**: Share your writing process, challenges, and triumphs with your audience. It's like leaving a

map for future writers to follow, showing them the path to success.

7. **Embrace Technology**: Use technology to your advantage, whether it's through self-publishing platforms, social media, or virtual events. It's like having a time machine, allowing you to reach readers across the globe.

The Legacy Extravaganza

Now, how do you blend these ingredients into a lasting legacy? It's all about creativity and a dash of humor. Imagine creating a series of books that each explore a different aspect of your literary universe. Or hosting a virtual event where you and other authors share your writing journeys. It's like a literary version of a family reunion, where each generation adds to the story.

The Aftermath

Once you've laid the foundation for your literary legacy, it's time to bask in the glory. You've just embarked on a journey that will continue long after your book is published. But don't forget to reflect on your achievements and set new goals. It's the literary equivalent of writing the next chapter in your story.

In conclusion, building a Literary Legacy is not just about writing a book; it's about creating a body of work that resonates with readers for generations. So, grab your pen, roll out the digital red carpet, and join the journey of building a Literary Legacy. Happy writing!

Chapter 25: The Self-Publishing Circus

In the grand circus of the literary world, self-publishing is the ultimate spectacle, a vibrant show where authors take center stage to share their stories with the world. But unlike traditional publishing, self-publishing is a DIY adventure that requires skill, creativity, and a bit of humor to navigate. So, how do you turn your self-publishing journey into a captivating performance? It's time to embark on the Self-Publishing Circus!

The Recipe for a Successful Self-Publishing Act

1. **Write a Stellar Book**: Like a circus performer who masters their craft, write a book that shines. Your story should be compelling, well-edited, and polished to perfection.

2. **Design an Eye-Catching Cover**: Your book cover is like the circus poster that attracts the crowd. Invest in a professional

design that grabs attention and reflects the essence of your story.

3. Format Your Book Like a Pro: Think of formatting as the stage setup. Whether it's eBook or print, ensure your book is formatted correctly for a seamless reading experience.

4. Price Your Book Strategically: Pricing is like setting the ticket price for your circus show. Research the market and price your book competitively to attract readers.

5. Market Your Book with Flair: Marketing is the ringmaster of your self-publishing circus. Use social media, email newsletters, and book promotions to create buzz and drive sales.

6. **Engage with Your Audience**: Your readers are the audience that keeps the circus going. Engage with them through social media, email, and in-person events.

7. **Collect Reviews and Testimonials**: Reviews are like applause after a great performance. Encourage readers to leave reviews and share their testimonials.

8. **Keep the Show Going**: Like a circus that travels from town to town, keep promoting your book across different platforms and audiences.

The Circus Performance

Now, how do you blend these ingredients into a self-publishing circus? It's all about creativity and a dash of humor. Imagine creating a series of humorous videos where you "interview" your book characters, or hosting a live Q&A session where you answer questions in character. It's like a literary version of a circus performance, but instead of a big top, you're using the internet.

The Aftermath

Once your self-publishing circus is in full swing, it's time to bask in the glory. You've just completed a digital performance where your book was the star, and self-publishing was your stage. But don't forget to track your sales, reviews, and audience feedback. It's the literary equivalent of a post-show analysis—a small gesture that goes a long way.

In conclusion, self-publishing is not just a business; it's a circus, a vibrant show where authors take center stage to share their stories with the world. So, grab your book, roll out the digital welcome mat, and join the Self-Publishing Circus. Happy performing!

Drew Wohlford always had dreams of becoming a scriptwriter but then life happened. His parents divorced shortly after high school, he attended St Francis College in Fort Wayne, Indiana after wandering aimlessly in life for years. Again he found his passion for writing being encouraged by Dr. L. Carl

Nadeau, his creative writing teacher.

Then life happened again, he met his wife, Brenda. Soon there were kids and then grandkids. There were numerous jobs of all kinds, as he tried to find his passion, but it had been put on a back burner. Then in November of 2020, Drew was hit with COVID-19, which turned into long COVID and without work, and facing his 60th birthday, Drew didn't look back, he looked forward and thought, it's now or never. With a laptop in hand, he began to document the stories he told his grandchildren. The passion had once again been ignited.

Discover These Other Great Books By Author Drew Wohlford on AMAZON

Discover These Other Great Books By Author Drew Wohlford on AMAZON

Discover These Other Great Books By Author Drew Wohlford on AMAZON

Discover These Other Great Books By Author Drew Wohlford on AMAZON

www.ingramcontent.com/pod-product-compliance
Lightning Source LLC
Chambersburg PA
CBHW052205220526
45471CB00004B/1829